OCEAN ANIMALS
A SEARCH AND FIND
BOOK FOR KIDS

Bethanie and Josh Hestermann
Illustrated by Sara Lynn Cramb

ROCKRIDGE
PRESS

To our curious, delightful Emma
—B.H. and J.H.

To my husband, Justin, for his limitless support and encouragement, and to all of the amazing animals that live on this planet, I am constantly awed and inspired by you
—S.L.C.

For general information on our other products and services or to obtain technical support, please contact our Customer Care Department within the United States at (866) 744-2665, or outside the United States at (510) 253-0500.

Rockridge Press publishes its books in a variety of electronic and print formats. Some content that appears in print may not be available in electronic books, and vice versa.

Interior and Cover Designer: Stephanie Sumulong
Art Producer: Janice Ackerman
Editor: Laura Bryn Sisson
Production Editor: Mia Moran

Custom Illustration © 2020 Sara Lynn Cramb

Author Photo: Genevieve Elaine Photography
Illustrator Photo: Justin Cramb

ISBN: Print 978-1-64611-512-9

R0

Contents

LET'S DIVE IN

Seen from space, our planet is mostly blue. Water covers more of its surface than land! The ocean is full of life. Its mountains, canyons, and even volcanoes are home to some amazing animals—from the tiniest creatures to the largest animal that has ever lived.

The ocean also has many secrets. In this book, you'll get to be an explorer and discover some of them. First, read about the animals and other things hidden on each page. Next, search for them in the picture. Want a challenge? Find the extra items, too!

As you search and find, you'll learn about ocean animals, their **habitats**, and what *you* can do to help keep the ocean healthy.

Ready to get started? Let's dive in!

Crab

Shrimp

Beach Umbrella

Seashell

Sandcastle

Surfer

Bottle of Reef–Safe Sunscreen

Seagull

Kite

Sunglasses

5

TIDE POOL

When the **tide** goes out, pockets of seawater called tide pools are sometimes left behind. Tide pools are full of living things—from spiky urchins and slimy seaweeds to very colorful slugs.

Giant Sea Star
Sea stars have five or more arms and many "tube feet" on their undersides. Little suckers on the tips of these tube feet keep sea stars from being washed away by waves.

Hermit Crab
Hermit crabs fold their soft bodies into empty seashells that they carry around wherever they go. As hermit crabs grow, they swap their smaller seashell homes for bigger ones.

Tidepool Sculpin

This little fish blends in and is hard to spot in a tide pool. If a tidepool sculpin gets trapped on land, it can breathe air while it tries to get back to seawater.

Keyhole Limpet

A keyhole limpet is a type of snail that breathes from the hole on top of its shell. Limpets use the very tiny, strong teeth on their tongues to scrape **algae** from rocks.

Nudibranch

No slug is fancier than a nudibranch (new-de-brank). These sea slugs don't have shells for protection, but their bright colors warn other animals that they taste bad.

Sea Lettuce

Many animals in tide pools eat sea lettuce, an algae that grows in the ocean. You could, too. Sea lettuce salad, anyone?

BONUS ROUND

Octopus

Red Sea Urchin

Sea Hare

Green Sea Anemone

TOUGHER THAN THE TIDE

Tide pool creatures must be tough enough to handle a lot of change as the tide goes in and out and in and out again.

SANDY SEAFLOOR

A sandy seafloor is the perfect home for animals like worms, crabs, and even flat fish that live in or on top of the sand. Sharks, rays, and other **predators** hunt here, often using their special senses to find food in the sand.

FIND LIFE IN THE SAND

Shovelnose Guitarfish
This guitar-shaped ray buries itself in the sand as it hunts. Its mouth is on its underside, so it can easily reach small fish, crabs, clams, worms, and other treats hiding in the seafloor.

Flounder
Both of a flounder's eyes are on the same side of its body, so it can lie flat and look up. The fish isn't born this way. One eye moves to join the other after birth.

Sea Cucumber

Sea cucumbers can protect themselves by shooting organs out of their bodies and regrowing them later. Predators get confused or tangled up in the mess while the sea cucumber gets away.

Spot Prawn

Can you imagine having five pairs of legs for walking and five *more* pairs for swimming, like a spot prawn? You will find this shrimp buried in the sandy seafloor.

Sand Dollar

Sand dollars look like fuzzy coins half buried in the sand. The fuzz is actually small spines that slowly move bits of food to the animal's mouth in the middle of its round body.

Cuttlefish

A cuttlefish hides by changing its skin color and pattern in the blink of an eye. It uses its eight arms and two tentacles to grab its **prey**.

MORE SAND DWELLERS

Big Skate

Grunt Sculpin

Brittle Star

Clam

WHAT IS SAND?

Most sand is made of tiny bits of rock, but some sand is parrotfish poop! Parrotfish eat coral, which comes back out as sand.

KELP FOREST

Tall seaweeds called kelp can grow hundreds of feet up from the ocean floor. These underwater forests provide food and shelter to animals like sea otters, sea urchins, and kelpfish. Each animal plays a role in keeping the kelp forest healthy.

WHO'S HIDING IN THE KELP?

Sea Otter
Cute, clever sea otters have armpit pockets for storing extra food and their favorite rocks. When resting, sea otters wrap themselves in kelp and hold hands to keep from floating away.

Sea Urchin
Sea urchins munch on kelp along the kelp forest floor. Sea otters, spiny lobsters, and other predators eat the urchins, keeping these spiny snackers from destroying too much kelp.

Harbor Seal

Harbor seals split their time between land and sea. They search for food underwater and can even nap there, but they come up for air every half hour.

Garibaldi

Did you see a flash of orange? It was probably a garibaldi. Garibaldis hide from predators, find food, lay eggs, and raise babies in the kelp forest.

Kelpfish

Spotted kelpfish can change colors to blend in with the kelp forest. Females lay eggs in nests attached to short seaweeds. Males guard the eggs until they hatch.

Giant Kelp

Giant kelp grows fast . . . up to two feet a day! Kelp anchors itself to the rocky seafloor and grows up, up, up. Air-filled sacs keep the kelp blades afloat.

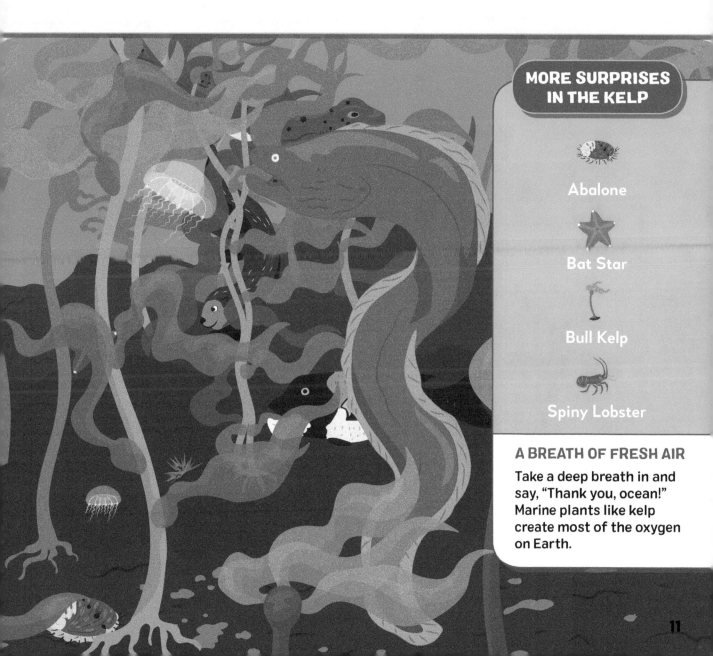

MORE SURPRISES IN THE KELP

Abalone

Bat Star

Bull Kelp

Spiny Lobster

A BREATH OF FRESH AIR

Take a deep breath in and say, "Thank you, ocean!" Marine plants like kelp create most of the oxygen on Earth.

OPEN OCEAN

The ocean stretches for miles and miles across the Earth. In some places, it's also miles and miles deep. What lives in all of that open space? Animals big and small spend time here, or just pass through as they travel from place to place.

Great White Shark
Great white sharks have strong jaws and rows of sharp teeth. When a tooth from the front row falls out, one from a back row takes its place. They never run out!

Pilot Whale
Pilot whales are black or dark gray with round heads. They dive deep for food like shrimps or eat small fish like herring. They live together in family groups.

Portuguese Man-of-War
A Portuguese man-of-war looks like a sea jelly, but it's actually a group of animals that live and work together. Those stinging tentacles can be more than 100 feet long.

Pilot Fish
Pilot fish hang around much bigger fish like sharks, eating their food scraps and cleaning their skin. To say thanks, sharks don't eat their pilot fish friends.

Blue Marlin
This large fish has a long, pointed bill that helps it catch prey. A blue marlin might swim so fast through a **school** of fish that it leaps right out of the water.

Ocean Sunfish
The ocean sunfish is flat and round and can weigh as much as a car. It's called a "sunfish" because it likes floating near the surface on its side, soaking in sunlight.

MORE SEAFARERS

Dolphinfish

Herring

Krill

Flying Fish

TINY TRAVELERS
Every night, millions of small animals called zooplankton travel from the deep sea to shallower waters to eat, and then go back before morning.

SHIPWRECK

When a ship sinks to the bottom of the sea, animals move right in. Humans like to explore shipwrecks by diving down with **SCUBA** gear. Can you imagine swimming around a sunken ship? What animals would you see? What treasures would you find?

Sand Tiger Shark
The sand tiger shark gulps air at the surface, making a bubble in its stomach. This air bubble helps the shark float above the seafloor, where it waits for its next meal.

Remora
A remora's fin acts like a suction cup. It sticks to a shark or other big fish and enjoys free meals, eating tiny animals called **parasites** off the shark's skin.

Moon Jelly

Like other sea jellies, a moon jelly is made mostly of water. It has no heart, brain, or even blood. Its mild sting stuns its tiny prey.

Smooth Butterfly Ray

A smooth butterfly ray feels smooth, almost slimy. Why? A layer of mucus (like the snot in your nose) covers and helps protect the ray's skin.

Gribble

These little critters are less than an inch long, but they can cause big trouble for wooden boats and docks. Gribbles dig into wood and eat it—like termites, but in the ocean.

Spotted Snake Eel

The spotted snake eel digs a burrow in the seafloor with its pointed tail. It spends most of its time buried there with its head sticking out, leaving at night to hunt for food.

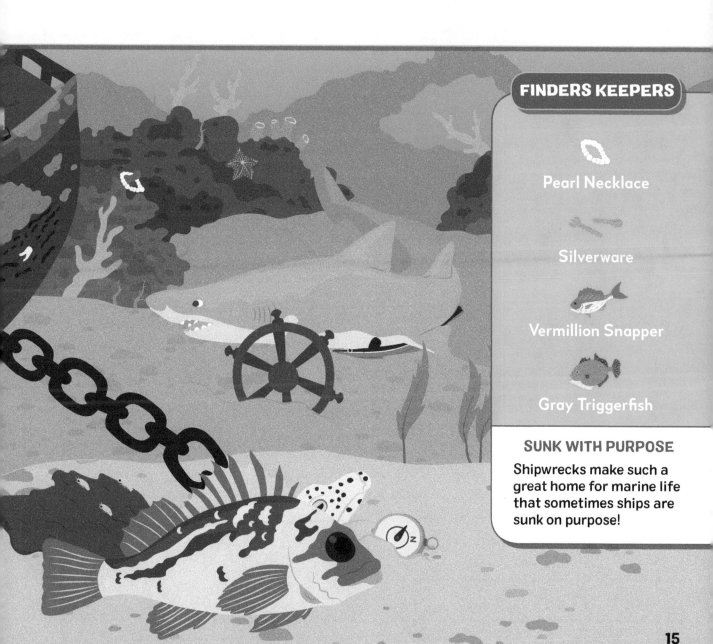

FINDERS KEEPERS

Pearl Necklace

Silverware

Vermillion Snapper

Gray Triggerfish

SUNK WITH PURPOSE

Shipwrecks make such a great home for marine life that sometimes ships are sunk on purpose!

DEEP SEA

The deep sea is dark, cold, and full of secrets. It's not a friendly place, but huge squids, fish with fangs, and many other surprising creatures live here. So much is left to learn about the deepest parts of the ocean. Now's your chance to explore!

CREEPERS OF THE DEEP

Anglerfish

A female anglerfish uses what looks like a glowing fishing pole sticking out of her head to trick her prey into coming closer. Then she eats it.

Blobfish

A blobfish's soft, blobby body is just right for living out its slow-paced life in the deep sea, thousands of feet below the surface.

Giant Squid

A giant squid can be as long as a bus, with eyes the size of beach balls that help it see in dark places. Its tentacles have sharp suckers on the ends.

Bloodybelly Comb Jelly

This jelly's color helps it blend into its dark habitat, because red looks black in the deep sea. The rows along its body are made of **cilia** that help it swim.

Dumbo Octopus

This octopus swims by flapping fins that look like floppy ears. It floats over the seafloor looking for food like worms and snails, swallowing them in one gulp.

Sperm Whale

Sperm whales dive thousands of feet down to hunt, sometimes holding their breath for more than an hour. They hunt and eat giant squid.

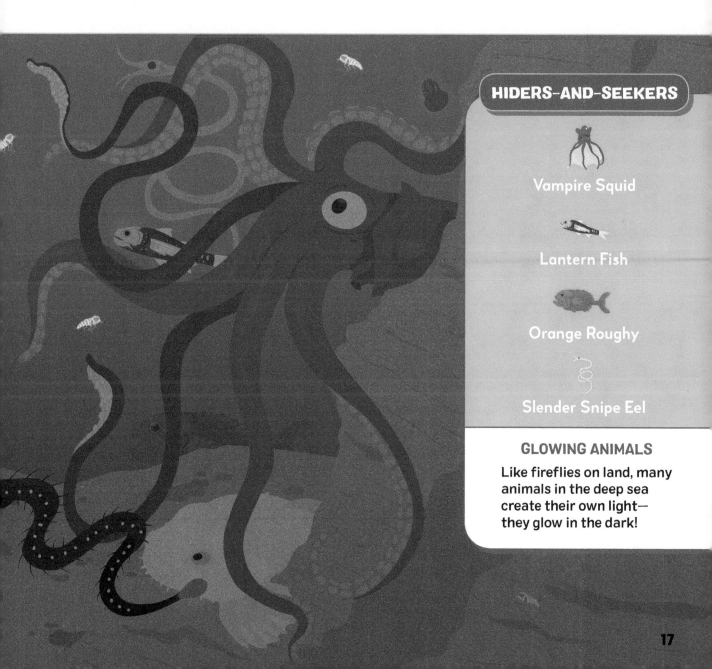

HIDERS-AND-SEEKERS

Vampire Squid

Lantern Fish

Orange Roughy

Slender Snipe Eel

GLOWING ANIMALS

Like fireflies on land, many animals in the deep sea create their own light— they glow in the dark!

HYDROTHERMAL VENT

A hydrothermal vent is like a fountain of hot water shooting out of a crack in the seafloor. This water can be hotter than 700°F. What could live in such a place? See what you can find!

VENT DWELLERS

Giant Tube Worm
Each vent worm lives inside a hard, white tube that can be taller than a human. They don't have mouths, but it kind of looks like they have red lips!

Vulcan Octopus
This vent octopus has see-through skin and may be blind. Vulcan octopuses like to hide in clumps of giant tube worms. They eat small shrimps and crabs.

Hydrothermal Vent Crab

These pale crabs live only around deep-sea vents. Their great sense of smell helps them find food like worms, clams, and mussels. Can you point one out?

Black Smoker

Hot water isn't the only thing coming out of deep-sea vents. **Minerals** mix with the cold seawater around deep-sea vents and turn solid. A black smoker spits out hot water and black minerals.

Zoarcid Fish

Vent zoarcid fish may snack on snails, shrimps, and even giant tube worms. They don't like to waste energy, so they move slowly.

White Smoker

White smokers are vents that let out hot water and white minerals. These vents look like chimneys puffing white smoke.

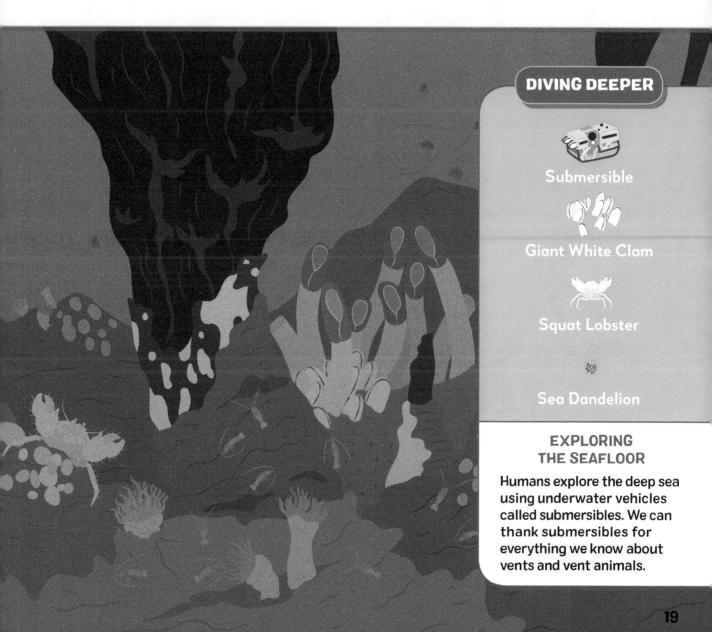

DIVING DEEPER

Submersible

Giant White Clam

Squat Lobster

Sea Dandelion

EXPLORING THE SEAFLOOR

Humans explore the deep sea using underwater vehicles called submersibles. We can thank submersibles for everything we know about vents and vent animals.

CORAL REEF

Coral reefs are like big cities in the sea. Thousands of animals gather around them to find food and hide from predators. Even the coral is alive! Corals can live for hundreds of years and come in every color of the rainbow. Reefs are truly wonderful worlds.

Clown Anemonefish
Clown anemonefish live among the tentacles of sea anemones. A layer of thick mucus protects a clownfish's skin from anemone stings. They help protect each other from predators.

Green Sea Turtle
Sea turtles have long flippers that help them swim. Unlike some other turtles, they can't pull their bodies into their shells. Green sea turtles come to coral reefs to eat algae.

Chambered Nautilus

A chambered nautilus has a round shell and about 90 tentacles it uses to grab prey. It zooms from place to place by pushing water through a tube near its head.

Brain Coral

Coral looks like rock, but it's actually a group of animals called polyps living together. Polyps have soft bodies surrounded by hard skeletons. Brain corals look like giant brains.

Spiny Puffer Fish

A puffer's spines usually lie flat. But when it's mad, it gulps seawater and puffs up like a prickly balloon. Then the spines stick straight out.

Hairy Frogfish

A hairy frogfish doesn't swim; it *walks* on its fins. Its long spines look like hair and help it blend in with the coral reef. Can you spot this strange animal?

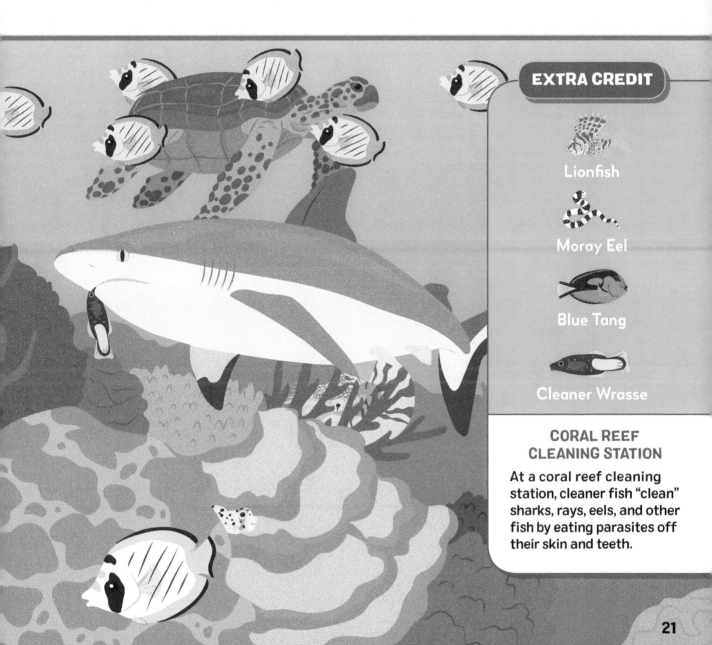

EXTRA CREDIT

Lionfish

Moray Eel

Blue Tang

Cleaner Wrasse

CORAL REEF CLEANING STATION

At a coral reef cleaning station, cleaner fish "clean" sharks, rays, eels, and other fish by eating parasites off their skin and teeth.

21

GREAT BARRIER REEF

The Great Barrier Reef off the coast of Australia is the biggest coral reef on Earth. It can be seen from outer space! Here, you'll find tiny seahorses, giant clams, huge manta rays, and maybe even a dugong (a cousin of the manatee).

Olive Sea Snake
The olive sea snake is a **venomous** reptile that surfaces to breathe. Its tail can sense light. This helps the snake know when its tail is sticking out of a hiding place.

Giant Clam
Giant clams can weigh more than 500 pounds and live 100 years or more. Each colorful clam is unique. When one chooses a spot on a reef, it attaches and stays there.

Humphead Wrasse

What coral reef fish has big lips and a bump on its forehead? A humphead wrasse! This large blue-green fish helps protect the Great Barrier Reef by eating crown-of-thorns sea stars.

Reef Stonefish

Is that a rock with eyes? No, it's a venomous reef stonefish! The stonefish uses **camouflage** to match the coral reef. It lies still until prey passes by, then gulps it down.

Giant Manta Ray

Giant mantas are the biggest rays in the ocean. They can be up to 29 feet wide. Mantas open their mouths as they swim, swallowing food like zooplankton as they go.

Parrotfish

Colorful parrotfish have strong teeth they use to munch on corals and eat algae off rocks. They tuck into a sleeping bag of mucus each night to protect themselves from predators.

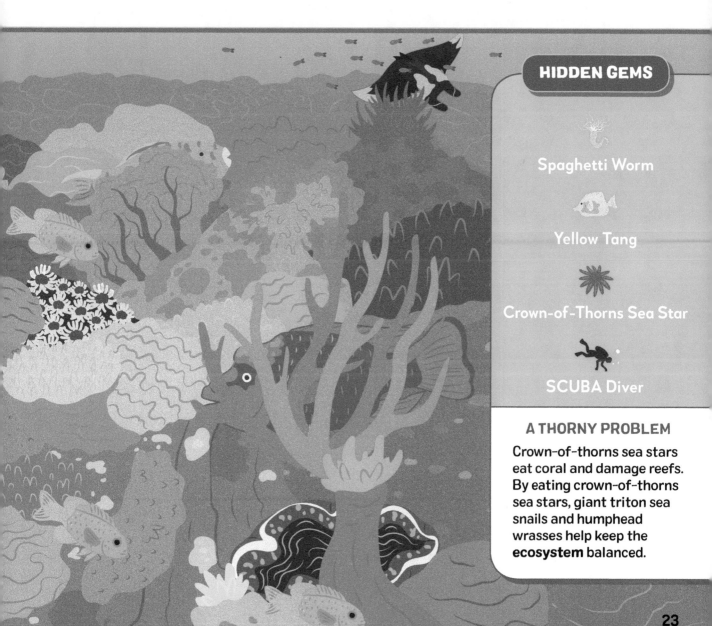

HIDDEN GEMS

Spaghetti Worm

Yellow Tang

Crown-of-Thorns Sea Star

SCUBA Diver

A THORNY PROBLEM

Crown-of-thorns sea stars eat coral and damage reefs. By eating crown-of-thorns sea stars, giant triton sea snails and humphead wrasses help keep the **ecosystem** balanced.

MANGROVE SWAMP

Mangrove trees grow along warm coastlines in salty seawater. Their underwater roots trap mud and sand, creating a unique habitat where many animals like to live. Predators like alligators and crocodiles are some of the biggest animals in a mangrove swamp. If you're lucky, you may even spot a panther.

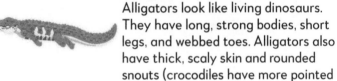

Alligator
Alligators look like living dinosaurs. They have long, strong bodies, short legs, and webbed toes. Alligators also have thick, scaly skin and rounded snouts (crocodiles have more pointed snouts).

Roseate Spoonbill
Do you see a pink bird? It's a roseate spoonbill. It digs for meals in the muddy seafloor with its spoon-shaped bill. A spoonbill's food turns it pink.

Great Blue Heron

The great blue heron has a long neck and blue-gray feathers. It uses its sharp beak to hunt in the swamp for fish. It builds nests with sticks and lays pale blue eggs.

Cane Toad

Humans brought this large, **poisonous** toad to the mangrove swamp, where it competes with other mangrove animals for food and space. It isn't supposed to be here, but it is!

Horseshoe Crab

A horseshoe crab is more like a spider than a crab. It has blue blood and 10 eyes! You can spot two big eyes on its U-shaped shell, and the rest look like small dots.

Diamondback Terrapin

This turtle lives on land and in water. Diamondback terrapins have webbed feet but no flippers and a diamond pattern on their shells.

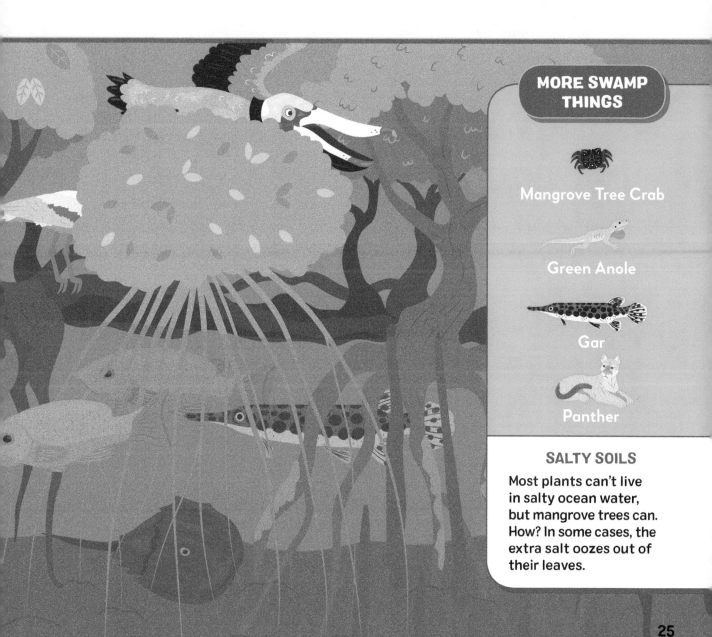

MORE SWAMP THINGS

Mangrove Tree Crab

Green Anole

Gar

Panther

SALTY SOILS

Most plants can't live in salty ocean water, but mangrove trees can. How? In some cases, the extra salt oozes out of their leaves.

SEAGRASS MEADOW

A seagrass meadow is a great place for baby animals to live, because there is plenty of food and shelter. Animals like the manatee and bonnethead shark visit these meadows to munch on seagrass. Others come to eat the small creatures that live in the seagrass.

Manatee
Manatees are called "sea cows," but they're actually related to elephants. Manatees move slowly, graze for hours, and sometimes eat 100 or more pounds of marine plants in one day.

Smalltooth Sawfish
This ray's nose looks like a saw. A smalltooth sawfish's "saw" helps it sense prey like shrimps and crabs along the seafloor—often in seagrass, sand, or mud.

Bonnethead Shark

Like other hammerhead sharks, bonnetheads have a strange head shape, kind of like a shovel. Bonnetheads eat seagrass as well as crabs, shrimps, and small fish.

Seahorse

Seahorses hold on to blades of seagrass with their tails to keep from floating away. They aren't good swimmers. Seahorse dads, not moms, carry and give birth to seahorse babies.

Trumpet Fish

A trumpet fish is long and thin. It floats vertically (up and down) to blend in with the seagrass. It opens its mouth wide and sucks food in like a vacuum.

Bottlenose Dolphin

Bottlenose dolphins hunt for large fish and squids in seagrass meadows. Dolphins use clicks, whistles, and squeaks to "talk" to one another and find food.

MORE IN THE MEADOW

Sea Hare

Queen Conch

Southern Stingray

Rainbow Parrotfish

DO ALL RAYS STING?

No. Only some rays, like the southern stingray, have a barb at the base of their tails that "stings" predators.

ARCTIC

The Arctic habitat includes the Arctic Ocean and the thick ice sheets that cover it as well as some land in places like Alaska, Canada, Greenland, Iceland, and Russia. Polar bears, seals, seabirds, and narwhals, the "unicorns of the sea," live near, on, or beneath the Arctic sea ice.

Polar Bear
Polar bears spend most of their lives on sea ice. Their skin is black, but they look white because their thick fur reflects sunlight. Even the bottoms of their feet have fur.

Walrus
Walruses have two long teeth called tusks and a layer of fat called blubber that keeps them warm in the cold Arctic. Their whiskers help them find food, like clams, on the seafloor.

Narwhal

A male narwhal has an almost 10-foot-long tusk sticking straight out of its lip. Can you see why its nickname is "unicorn of the sea"?

Beluga

Baby belugas are born gray and turn white as they grow, which helps them match their icy Arctic habitat. The round bump on a beluga's head is called a melon.

Puffin

Puffins spend a lot of time at sea. They fly over the ocean, rest on the surface, and dive to catch fish. Many puffins build nests and lay eggs in Iceland.

Arctic Fox

An Arctic fox's fur is gray in the summer and white in the winter. When food is hard to find, the fox may follow a polar bear and eat its leftovers.

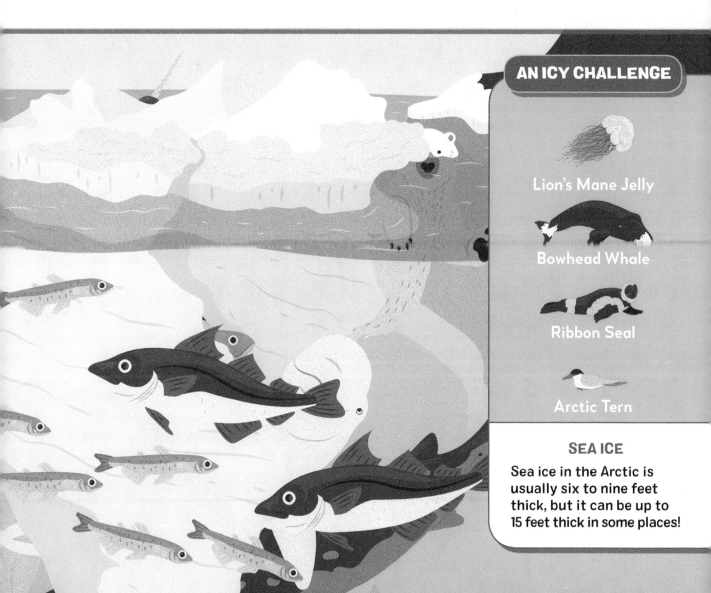

AN ICY CHALLENGE

Lion's Mane Jelly

Bowhead Whale

Ribbon Seal

Arctic Tern

SEA ICE

Sea ice in the Arctic is usually six to nine feet thick, but it can be up to 15 feet thick in some places!

ANTARCTIC

The Antarctic is made up of Antarctica and the icy waters of the Southern Ocean. It's very cold, windy, and dry. Antarctica is actually a desert covered by ice! It's the coldest place on Earth—winter temperatures can drop below −100°F.

Elephant Seal
A male elephant seal's long nose looks like an elephant's trunk. Males can be 20 feet long and weigh 8,000 pounds or more.

Emperor Penguin
Penguins are birds that can't fly. To stay warm on the ice, emperor penguins huddle together, taking turns standing on the outside so no one penguin gets too cold.

Leopard Seal

These tough, slender seals live on the sea ice surrounding Antarctica, hunting penguins, squids, fish, and even other seals. Their only predator is the orca.

Crocodile Icefish

The crocodile icefish has white blood and a long snout like a crocodile's. It lives in the cold Southern Ocean.

Blue Whale

Blue whales are the loudest animals on Earth. They're also the biggest—even bigger than dinosaurs were! These ocean giants eat up to four tons of krill every day.

Orca

These black-and-white dolphins are often called "killer whales." Orcas and other dolphins are some of the smartest animals on Earth. They live and hunt in small groups called pods.

ANTARCTIC, ROUND 2

Wandering Albatross

Antarctic Krill

Adelie Penguin

Antarctic Sea Jelly

NORTH POLE VS. SOUTH POLE

Here's a fun fact: Penguins and polar bears don't live together. Polar bears live in the North Pole, and penguins live in the South Pole.

COASTLINE

Most of the ocean is far away from land, but there are more animals living near coasts than anywhere else in the sea. Some animals stay near the same shore their whole lives. Others, like the gray whale, come and go as they **migrate** from one place to another.

Sea Lion
Sea lions are curious, playful, and smart—like dogs with flippers. They even make a noise that sounds like barking! Sea lions live close to coasts and spend time on land and in the sea.

Whale Shark
Is that a whale or a shark? It's a shark, and it's about the size of a school bus. Toothlike scales cover a whale shark's spotted body.

Mexican Fishing Bat

This fuzzy brown bat sleeps on land during the day and then flies out at night to hunt for fish in the ocean.

Osprey

An osprey has a dark brown and white body, sharp, curved toenails called talons, and yellow eyes. Ospreys build stick nests high up in trees. They dive into the ocean to catch fish.

Gray Whale

Gray whales eat small animals that live on or in the seafloor. They travel long distances but stay close to coasts. A gray whale breathes air through two holes on top of its head.

Barnacle

Barnacles glue themselves to rocks or other surfaces, then reach out with their feathery legs to collect food as it floats by. Some barnacles live on other animals. Can you find one?

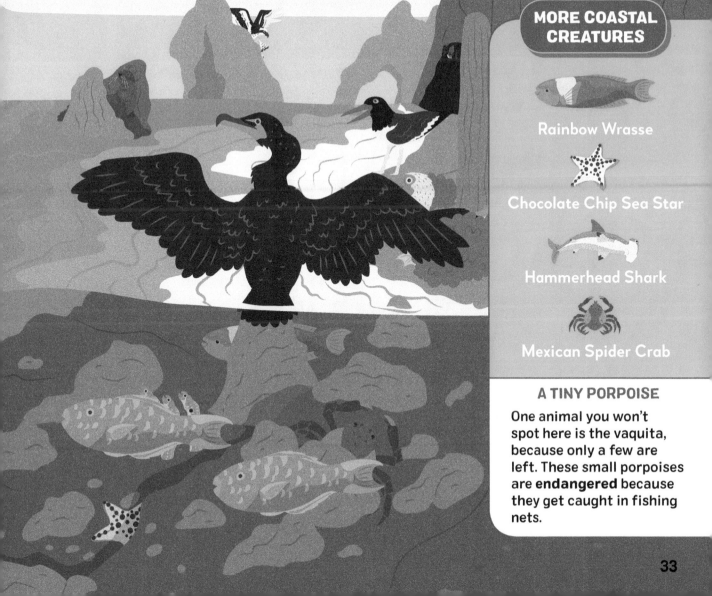

MORE COASTAL CREATURES

Rainbow Wrasse

Chocolate Chip Sea Star

Hammerhead Shark

Mexican Spider Crab

A TINY PORPOISE

One animal you won't spot here is the vaquita, because only a few are left. These small porpoises are **endangered** because they get caught in fishing nets.

HOW YOU CAN HELP

Now that you have learned a lot about the ocean, you know how important it is. But the ocean is in danger.

Pollution is a big problem, even at sea. Humans create tons of trash, and some of it ends up in the ocean, where animals may think it's food. Having plastic in their stomachs can make animals very sick.

The ocean is also getting warmer, melting the sea ice that many polar animals depend on to live. Warmer seawater can hurt coral reefs, too. Corals turn white and die when ocean conditions change too much.

Some animals on this page don't live together in the wild, but they all depend on the ocean, and many of them are endangered. Here are some simple ways your family can help:

Reduce: Use less plastic. Bring reusable bags to the grocery store and say no to plastic straws.

Reuse: Buy used toys or clothes instead of new ones.

Recycle: Put paper, cardboard, glass bottles, and cans in the recycling bin.

Find 10 pieces of litter to help clean up the ocean.

Shoe

Fishing Net

Take-Out Food Container

Six-Pack Rings

Balloon

Plastic Bag

Soda Can

Plastic Straw

Beach Toy

Water Bottle

Answer Key

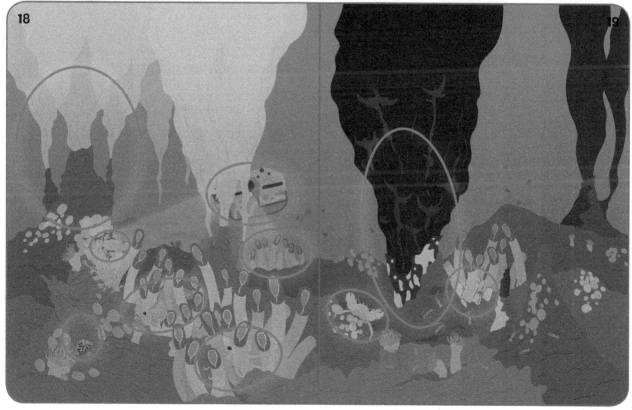

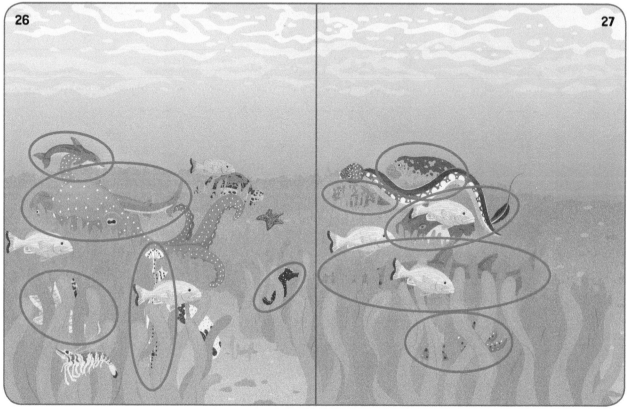

Glossary

algae: Plantlike organisms (living things) that live in water and get energy from the sun

camouflage: The ability to blend in by matching the background

cilia: Tiny hairlike structures that move back and forth

ecosystem: A community of plants and animals living together

endangered: At risk of going extinct and disappearing from the wild

habitat: The place an animal lives

migrate: Travel from one place to another

mineral: A nonliving material that comes from the Earth and makes up rocks and soil

parasite: An organism that lives off of another organism

poisonous: Something that can be harmful if touched or eaten

pollution: Harmful items like trash and plastic waste, as well as gases, chemicals, and oils, that humans add to the environment

predator: An animal that eats other animals for food

prey: An animal that other animals eat for food

school: A group of fish

SCUBA: Gear that allows humans to breathe underwater

tide: The rise and fall of the ocean, usually twice a day

venomous: An animal that uses a harmful substance called venom to injure other animals, usually by bite or sting

About the Authors

Bethanie and Josh Hestermann are authors of animal science books for kids. They wrote *Zoo Animals: A Search and Find Book for Kids*, as well as *Zoology for Kids* and *Marine Science for Kids* for advanced readers (ages 9+). Bethanie is a freelance writer, and Josh is a zoologist working at the California Science Center. They live in Southern California with their two kids.

About the Illustrator

Sara Lynn Cramb illustrates educational books for kids. She has created illustrations for many titles, including *Zoo Animals: A Search and Find Book for Kids*, *Animals of the World: A Lift-the-Flap Book*, and *Out and About: Night Explorer*. Sara loves creating work that excites and educates kids about the natural world.

CPSIA information can be obtained
at www.ICGtesting.com
Printed in the USA
LVHW020403100420
652666LV00004B/4

9 781646 115129